GH00538450

THE ILLUSTRATED MOTORCYCLE LEGENDS

Yamaha

ROY BACON

SUNBURST BOOKS

This edition published in 1996 by
Sunburst Books
Kiln House, 210 New Kings Road
London SW6 4NZ

© Text Roy Bacon 1996
© Layout and Design the Promotional Reprint Company Ltd 1996

ISBN 1 85778 213 5

ACKNOWLEDGEMENTS

The author and publishers wish to acknowledge their debt to Yamaha, whose material has
provided the bulk of the pictures used in this title. Most have been collected by the author
over the years; others were sent on request to complete the story.

FRONT COVER AND TITLE PAGE :
The XTZ750 Super Ténéré twin-cylinder trail model as for 1995.

BACK COVER:
The mighty XVZ1300A Royal Star of 1996; massive V-four engine, traditional style and
modern technology.

Every effort has been made to trace the ownership of all copyrighted material and
to secure permission from copyright holders. In the event of any question arising
as to the use of any material, we will be pleased to make necessary corrections in
future printings.

Printed and bound in China

Contents

Music and Motorcycles 1851-1967   *4*

Off-road and XS 1968-1974   *8*

Monoshock 1975-1979   *16*

Elsie, XJ and Virago 1980-1984   *29*

Five Valves and V-max 1985-1986   *46*

Genesis and Deltabox 1987-1992   *50*

Omega and Retro 1993-1996   *65*

Yamaha Models   *79*

MUSIC AND MOTORCYCLES 1851-1967

Yamaha: the firm whose trademark of three tuning forks highlights its musical origins. The whole story began in 1851, when Torakusu Yamaha was born, for he was later to show an aptitude for engineering and to complete two apprenticeships, one in clock-making, the other in medical equipment.

These skills enabled him to repair an organ which he had been asked to look at – a chance happening which inspired him to build one himself – and so the Yamaha Musical Instrument Company was set up, prospered, joined together with others, and became the Nippon Gakki Company. It became one of the world's largest in its field but fell on hard times in the 1920s and 1930s before making a slow recovery in the late 1940s. The firm's continuous search for new products eventually led to the sphere of transport and in 1954 it began to design a motorcycle, despite the many Japanese marques already in business.

The start of the Yamaha line was this YA1, built in 1955 and known as the Red Dragonfly.

Early days yet – but by 1957 the 125 had a spine frame while the 250 twin was being exported.

Lacking motorcycle experience and seeking to build a small-capacity, high-quality product, Yamaha chose to copy the DKW RT125, just as BSA, Harley-Davidson and Voskhod had done before them, and this proved to be a wise decision. They added a fourth speed in the gearbox of the 125cc two-stroke engine and adopted gear primary drive. It was coded YA1 but was to be known as the Red Dragonfly because of its finish.

The machine was an immediate success, partly thanks to race wins at the Mount Fuji and Asama events of 1955, and was quickly joined by the 175cc YC1 and, in 1957, the 247cc YD1 twin. This too was based on a German machine, the Adler, but the design team were now allowed more freedom to incorporate their own ideas. The result was a further success and Yamaha expanded as a motorcycle firm, took over others, and began to look outside their homeland to new markets.

Sonny Angel of the United States raced this Yamaha at Silverstone in 1960. A YDS1 fitted with a race kit, it was off the pace.

By 1971 the road-racing twins had become the 250cc TD2B and 350cc TR2B. They were fast, reliable and successful.

For this they needed publicity and began by racing a twin at Catalina Island in the United States in 1958. They returned to Asama the next year, noted the speed of the Showa, which used a disc-valve, two-stroke engine, took over Showa and adopted that engine type for their debut race in Europe in 1961, the French GP. From that start came a 250cc world title in 1964, the first of several which were gained in that decade.

Considerably earlier than this, the Yamaha name had become known in both Europe and America as a manufacturer of motorcycles fitted with two-stroke engines of power and quality. While there were some excellent singles, it was the twins that really captured the attention, for the YD series proved to be a high-performer and well-equipped in the style that was quickly found to be the norm with Japanese machines.

Alongside the road twins there were competition versions. These were the DS street scrambler, sold in the United States as the Ascot, and the first of the TD and TR racing models. These transformed the road racing scene by the end of the 1960s, for they became both fast and reliable.

An early single, the 80/G1F, which was much as other models with spine frame and Autolube lubrication for the engine.

Yamaha joined the scooterette boom using a two-stroke engine driving a three-speed gearbox.

One of the small twins, the 200/CS3E of 1971, which had five speeds.

The 250cc YDS3 of 1965, showing the fine detailing of the early twins. Good for over 130 km/h (80 mph).

On the road, the Yamaha range settled down to small-capacity singles, a scooterette, very neat 100cc and 125cc twins, the 250cc twins and, in 1967, a 350cc twin. This last was a technical step forward, for it had a horizontally-split crankcase, into one half of which all of the shafts and the bearings were dropped and then held by the other half. It was also a move away from the many small models Yamaha had built up to then, always concentrating on the lightweight market and selling most of them close to home rather than into the markets of the United States and Europe, who saw a relatively small part of their total range. This was about to change.

Off-road, Yamaha continued to build street-scramblers based on road twins up to the end of the 1960s, but these had few changes other than upswept pipes, so they were only suited to gentle trail riding. However, their power did give them speed over hard-packed surfaces and they looked good, so they sold well.

In the United States, two types of off-road machine were in use, one for desert racing, the other for enduros in the north-eastern states. The desert sleds, usually twins, demanded brute power and stability from the machines and strength from the rider to control the weight. The enduros called for less weight, quick steering and low-down power, so were much as trials models and used a smaller engine, usually a two-stroke single.

Yamaha saw that there was a major market for a dual-purpose machine, one able to perform well on the road but equally able to run off-road for fun or in competition. Thus came the trail machine, which was able to compete in enduros or simply take its owner up to the hills for the view. Small, light and handy, it could go many places without tiring the rider and Yamaha's first was the DT1 of 1968, powered by a 246cc two-stroke single driving a five-speed gearbox. It was the start of a long, and most successful, off-road line.

An early trail model which opened up a whole new market for motorcycling, the 1973 125/AT3 five-speed machine.

A later DT175 machine from 1979, by which time it featured the Yamaha monoshock rear suspension.

The first four-stroke was the XS1, which had a 653cc parallel-twin, overhead-camshaft engine, and was introduced in 1970.

The rotary-engine Yanmar RZ201, here seen on show in Japan, was fated never to go into production.

Twin overhead camshafts and an inclined engine distinguished the XS500 from the larger twin.

side seat is extra comfortable to help riding fatigue when the bike is continuously for long periods. ...ned for the best riding posture, the ...ends in with the dynamic lines of

IC Regulator
To assure that the charging current to the battery is maintained at a correct level, an integrated-circuit (IC) feedback amplifier is used for the regulator circuit. Unlike conventional breaker-type systems, this IC regulator requires no maintenance and has

Engine
The new XS500 is powered by a 4-stroke, parallel-twin engine with a double-overhead-cam system driving eight valves to assure maximum intake and exhaust efficiency. Fed by a pair of constant-vacuum carburetors, this DOHC engine is highly responsive yielding an optimum acceleration curve across the entire speed range of the machine, and to drastically reduce

Water-cooling turned the racing twin into the highly-successful TZ250 and TZ350. Later came the TZ fours.

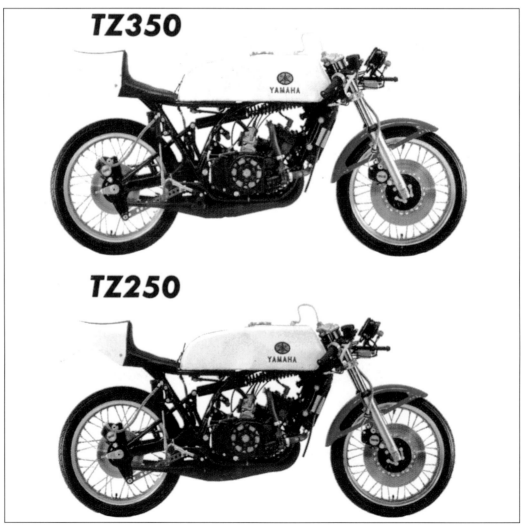

Within a couple of years there were further trail models of 125, 175 and 360cc, but the firm's next step was unexpected, for in 1970 they produced their first four-stroke model, the XS1. This took them firmly into Triumph and Honda territory with a 653cc vertical twin, overhead-camshaft model using knowledge they had gained from Hosk, a firm that came to them with Showa. Whereas the latter had introduced them to two-stroke engines with disc valves, the Hosk line included a 500cc ohc twin which was capable of 110mph and well able to run with some of the best from Britain .

The XS1 was not as quick as the Hosk and lacked its character but was a more civilised machine. It led on to the XS2 of 1972, when it was joined by two short-lived models. The first of these was the TX750, a vertical twin which introduced balance shafts within the crankcase to reduce vibration. The system was known as 'Omni-Phase Balancer' and worked well, but the machine proved unreliable and was quickly dropped. The second model, which never reached production, had a 662cc rotary Yanmar twin engine and was only seen at Tokyo shows. In 1973 the TX500 appeared with twin overhead camshafts and two years later evolved into the XS500 which sold to the end of the decade, but never in large numbers.

Fizzie, as the FS1E was known to most owners, developed into this FS1DX with disc brake by 1980.

The simple YB100 was much as Yamaha's early singles and remained in production into the 1990s.

On the two-stroke front, Yamaha had learned that water-cooling was vital for a high-powered engine if it was to be reliable and maintain power output for long periods. This led to the racing TZ series which was based at first on the twins in 250 and 350cc sizes and destined to become the private owners' standby and one of the most successful machines of all time. Later came fours of 500 and 700 or 750cc used for solo and sidecar racing, but it was the twins, and a 125cc single, that were the main production.

At the other end of the scale, 1973 saw the introduction of the FS1E, soon known as 'Fizzie' to its teenage market, on which so many took their first motorcycling steps. In Britain it was classed as a moped, since it had a 50cc engine and pedals, but the latter folded to act as footrests and it had a sporting performance and image.

The same applied to the larger YB100 which was similar in that it had a disc-valve two-stroke engine and four-speed gearbox, simple construction, and was to run on into the 1990s offering basic transport, adequate performance and minimal running costs. The twins changed their model codes to become RD125, RD200, RD250 and RD350, all similar and the codes easier to follow than before. In much the same way, the trail models became the DT series using the letters plus the capacity so the original DT1 was the DT250.

From 1973 the two-stroke twins became the RD series, indicating that they were Race Developed. The smallest was this RD125.

Next in the RD-line came the RD200 – this particular model dates from 1981.

Continuing the style and line was the RD250, perhaps the most popular machine of this series.

Largest in 1973 was the RD350, later to be stretched to the RD400 (below).

RD350

An offshoot of the trail models was the AG100 Ag-Bike which was built for use on farms, ranches and in the outback. For this machine, the stock model was modified to improve the off-road features, by adding guards to protect the rider's feet and hands, enclosing the chain and fitting front and rear carriers. Ideal for its task, it remained in production for many years.

To supplement the trail models came the MX series for motocross use at novice and junior level, quickly followed by the YZ machines for more serious work. The first, built in 100, 125, 250, 360 and, finally, 400cc capacities, was built to a price and kept the Autolube oil pump from the road and trail series, plus the Omni-Phase balancer as in the TX750. Yamaha expected it to be the main seller but soon found that buyers wanted the YZ which was more suited to racing, albeit at a price. Most of the MX models had gone by 1976, just the MX100 hanging on until 1980, but the YZ ran on and on, with a 125 joining the 250 and 360 for 1974.

One of the trail models was this DT100, which used the firm's technology effectively on a small scale.

An offshoot of the trail model was this AG100, designed for use when working over wide-open spaces.

The MX250 was one of a series of similar models built to a price for casual use.

For serious racing there was the YZ series, built in several sizes including this 125, and preferred by the buying public.

MONOSHOCK 1975-1979

It was in 1975 that the motocross models began to adopt the monoshock rear suspension system first seen on the works machines. In order to improve wheel travel and suspension unit life, Yamaha fitted a single, long shock absorber above the engine. This was fixed to the headstock at the front, and at the rear to a triangulated fork. It was a system used by the TZ road racers in 1976 and by more and more models over the years.

That year the utilitarian YB100 was joined by the five-speed RS100, a machine which had a superior chassis, as did the larger RS125 – both to be offered for a decade. A range of true trials models was introduced as the TY80, TY175 and TY250 while the trail series was extended to the DT400. The larger four-stroke twin changed its code to XS650 while the smaller, still with its twin camshafts and Omni-Phase balancer, became the eight-valve XS500.

The largest two-stroke twin was stretched to become the RD400 for 1976, a year when most Yamaha news was off-road. The YZ100 and YZ400 models extended the motocross line, which was joined by an enduro model. This was the IT400, which was essentially the YZ400 with the addition of lights and a change of fittings to make it street-legal.

The RS100 was introduced for 1976 to offer a little more than the basic YB100.

The RS125, which was built for a decade and shared its chassis with the RS100.

The smallest model for trials use in 1976 was the TY80, which followed the lines of the series (below).

The mid-range trials model was the TY175, light and easy to handle.

The largest of the trials range was the TY250, which offered a little more capacity and power.

The DT400 extended the trail-model series while offering a useful performance on the road (above).

The original four-stroke twin became the XS650 in 1976, developed rather than radically altered.

In 1976 the largest two-stroke twin grew to become the RD400, offering ever more performance.

The YZ100 motocross model was added in 1976 for the junior rider (near right).

The YZ400 was serious motocross business but with added lights could become the IT400 enduro model.

An overhead-camshaft, single-cylinder engine powered the XT500 trail model in a manner from the past (near left).

Completely different was the XT500, for this had a single-cylinder, overhead-camshaft, four-stroke engine to offer an alternative trail model, well able to comply with the ever-more-stringent emission laws in the United States. The result was a totally different form of power output, well able to climb most hills and easy to ride. It made a fine dual-purpose model and Yamaha also listed a pure off-road version, the TT500, stripped for action although not an enduro model.

Both road and off-road ranges expanded for 1977, the latter seeing the trials TY50, motocross YZ80 and enduro IT175 and IT250 models added. For the road there were two vertical twins and a triple. The twins were the XS250 and XS400, both derived from a short-lived XS360 and with much in common. Their engines had a single overhead camshaft, conventional construction and drove six-speed gearboxes. Inevitably, the smaller suffered from the weight it had to carry but both performed adequately in their class.

The triple, listed as the XS750, had three cylinders set across the frame, twin overhead camshafts, five speeds and shaft final drive, then a rare feature other than for a BMW. It was a long-distance tourer and did this job well.

The XS750 was joined in 1978 by the XS1100, which stretched the triple to four cylinders while keeping its main features. It was still a tourer, but a powerful one able to exceed 220 km/h (130 mph) and best suited to the long roads of the United States. In Europe, its weight and slow handling told against it for sports riders, but its power remained for high-speed cruising.

The logical partner to the XT500 also appeared in 1978 as the road model SR500. It used the same engine in cycle parts modified for road use and was listed for some years. There was also the HL500, which was built in Europe in small numbers as a production version of a factory motocross model using a tuned TT500 engine in a replica factory chassis, but this proved not to be a success. Two more 50cc models were added at the bottom end of the scale, the RD50 for the road and the DT50 for the trail.

Stripped for more serious action, the big single became the TT500.

Smallest trials model was this TY50, first seen in 1977, and continuing the style of the type.

Two four-stroke, overhead-camshaft twins appeared for 1977: the XS250 and this XS400, which shared its chassis.

XS400

In 1977, the XS750 – a triple – offered twin overhead camshafts and shaft drive for touring (above).

The triple was joined in 1978 by the 130mph XS1100 four, a very high-speed cruiser.

Developed from the XT500, the SR500 was a logical model and was introduced in 1978 for road use.

This HL500 was based on a factory motocross model, used a tuned TT500 engine, and was built in Europe.

In 1979 Yamaha had their first look at the custom market with the XS650SE or Special. This was styled for the United States with high bars, stepped seat, cast-alloy wheels, 16-inch rear tyre and small tank, but was essentially the stock model. It was joined by three similarly-styled machines for 1980, these being the XS250SE, XS400SE and XS750SE, all with the same features. For those who preferred that style with a single cylinder there was the SR250 which had an overhead camshaft engine and five speeds but retained the wire-spoked wheels.

The RD style was taken right down to the smallest model, as this RD50 shows with its alloy wheels and disc brake.

For the trail rider there was the DT50, again with the style and fitments of the larger models.

The XS650SE Special first appeared in 1979 and was aimed at the custom market, with wheels, tank, seat and bars to suit.

The custom range extended for 1980 using the existing models as a starting point. The smallest was this XS250SE.

Mid-range custom was covered by this XS400SE, again based on the road twin.

The triple turned into the XS750SE with the same style, lines and fittings (above).

There was also a custom single, the SR250SE, which repeated the exercise in its own way.

ELSIE, XJ AND VIRAGO 1980-1984

Two of the most popular of all Yamaha models appeared in 1980, the water-cooled RD250LC and its 350 equivalent. These were unexpected, for the air-cooled RD twins had fallen victim to the emission laws of the United States, despite some very clever technical work which resulted in the RD400F of 1979. The LC series, quickly dubbed 'Elsie', changed this situation and introduced some of the most exciting motorcycles of all time, a reminder of earlier days when 'ring-ding' two strokes were less civilised and much more fun.

The style was that of the TZ racer with matt-black engine finish, slim fuel tank and monoshock rear suspension. Along with this went much of the racing machine's technology, amended for street use, but in a manner which made it run like a racer on the road. It was not, perhaps, a machine for casual riding, but responded well when driven to suit its power delivery. The two models sold well and in 1981 a Pro-Am race series was devised for them and produced some of the most exciting racing of all time. Any LC was always fun to ride. In addition to the new twins there was the RS200 – a model which took the RS125 single style but fitted a twin-cylinder engine to make a neat package.

The smaller of the two Elsie models, the water-cooled RD250LC, which looked and behaved like a racer.

The larger RD350LC shared many parts with the above model and went on to this later version with many improvements.

There were also two new four-stroke models for 1980, one the XS850 which was a stretched XS750 triple with larger carburettors and other improvements to boost its performance. The second new model, the XJ650, introduced a new and narrower engine type with the electrics mounted behind the cylinders and above the gearbox. In most other respects the details of the XS-series were used so the four cylinders had twin overhead camshafts and the engine drove a five-speed gearbox connected to shaft final drive. Disc brakes and cast-alloy wheels completed a style of the time.

On the trail the range extended to add the IT125, IT425 and XT250, the last using a 249cc single-cylinder, overhead-camshaft engine. Away from the motorcycles, the firm added the Passola scooter to its line to supplement the long-running scooterette V50 and V80 models. Automatic in many ways, it was aimed at the shopping and commuter market. The 72cc Chappy joined it the next year with more of a sports style while keeping the small wheels.

The small twin returned as the RS200, which had the style of the singles.

Stretched from the earlier triple, the XS850 of 1980 had a boost in its performance.

New and slimmer for 1980 was this XJ650, which introduced a whole series.

A smaller trail single, the XT250 retained the overhead camshaft engine and style of the XT500.

The Passola scooter joined the scooterette range for 1980: simple, automatic, and easy to ride.

The V50 scooterette which was built in V75, V80 and V90 forms over the years.

Another scooter form was the Chappy in more sporting style.

The massive IT465 enduro model, enlarged from the earlier 425, and essentially motocross with lights.

Water-cooling enhanced the YZ125's performance and was later used by the rest of that series.

An economy twin, ideal for the ride to work, the XS250C kept the single-camshaft engine.

The 1981 list added more trail models in the form of the DT80 and the IT465, the latter being a further stretch of the largest engine in the series. The big trail single became the larger XT550 and was fitted with a four-valve head and twin carburettors, one for each of the two inlet valves, but of different types. The effect was to improve the pick-up and running right through the range, and the model used the monoshock frame. The YZ125 gained water-cooling, something which was to spread through that range over the years. On the road there was the XS250C, an economy model having five speeds, wire wheels and drum brakes while the XS1100 was offered in sports form with a fairing and this could be had as a limited edition, in Martini colours.

The new line of fours was extended with the addition of the XJ550, while there were further mopeds and a pair of models having V-twin engines. The XV750SE, known as the Virago, had a 748cc, overhead-camshaft engine, five speeds and shaft drive in a custom style much as the other SE models but with monoshock rear suspension. The TR1 was much the same but enlarged to 981cc with chain final drive, while both were best suited to highway cruising in the United States, their prime market.

A whole range of new models appeared for 1982, headed by the XJ650 Turbo. It was a time when all four Japanese firms tried the turbo-charged engine route to more sales, but all found it a complex solution to a problem best solved by more capacity. None of the models were listed for long and they failed to sell in significant numbers.

Sport version of the XS1100 as produced in 1980, for the next year the twin spots were dropped.

The four range was extended to add the XJ750 in the style of the others, while the XS400 went into a monoshock frame. The XZ550 was another V-twin, but in the European style with a water-cooled engine, twin overhead camshafts, four-valve heads, five speeds and shaft drive. Sadly, this machine was to prove a poor performer and none too reliable, so it had a short model life.

The other new models were smaller with the off-road XT125 and XT200 trail and custom SR125SE road models both using an overhead camshaft engine. Two-stroke power was used for the water-cooled, off-road DT125LC and the road RD125LC. The latter copied the style of the larger Elsie twins and was available in full-power or learner-restricted forms. Smaller but similar were the RD80LC and economy RD80MX, the first of which was another machine in the Elsie mould, and the second featured wire wheels and air-cooled engine. The scooter range was also extended with the CV80 Beluga in a similar style to the Passola which gained electric start; and the motocross YZ80 and YZ250 gained the water-cooling system.

The XJ550 of the 1981 list extended the slimmer line of four-cylinder models and performed well.

The QT50 – a basic moped, but featuring shaft drive for minimal maintenance.

The Bop II moped had leg shields and two speeds but kept the shaft drive.

A V-twin, overhead-camshaft engine was introduced for the custom-styled XV750SE which became known as the Virago.

The TR1 was a larger V-twin with chain drive and a more European style.

Turbo power was tried for 1982, the XJ650 being the model Yamaha chose for this treatment.

One of the firm's long-running models appeared in 1983. This was the XJ900, which continued the series' sports theme. Thus, it was slim and light, powered by a four-cylinder, twin-cam engine, and had five speeds and shaft drive. Its one problem area lay with a handlebar-mounted fairing which made it weave badly at high speed. Within a year the culprit was replaced by a larger fairing fixed to the frame and the model than sold steadily into the next decade.

For the United States, the firm introduced a fully-equipped tourer, the XVZ12TD Venture. Powered by 1198cc water-cooled, V-4 engine having twin overhead camshafts, the model was a full dresser with fairing, panniers, top box and radio for cruising down the highway in California, or any other of the states. The five speeds and shaft drive were expected, but there was also a linked braking system and self-levelling suspension.

A superior model was the XJ750 four which continued the slim style of the series.

The XZ550 V-twin was a technical step forward with water-cooling and four-valve heads but was not a commercial success.

Towards the other end of the scale, the RXS100 took over the 100cc commuter role, with the engine incorporating some technical improvements originating from the motocross models. Smaller still was the T80 Town Mate scooterette which continued the long and successful series, but with a four-stroke engine and shaft drive. Additionally, in the off-road category, two more models were added as the IT250 and the IT490.

The XJ600 appeared in 1984 to replace both the XJ550 and XJ650 for what was to become the middleweight class. In the United States of America it was initially listed as the FJ600 and in the same way the RD350LC was sold there as the RZ350. It was joined by the FJ1100, with a slim, four-cylinder, twin-cam, 16-valve engine installed in a new type of frame with the main loops running either side of the engine. The suspension was sophisticated and a fairing and belly pan aided the airflow over rider and machine.

A smaller four-stroke trail model for 1982 was the XT125, which was introduced along with the XT200.

The custom style went down to a smaller size with the SR125 of 1982, which had all of the expected features.

PHOTO: PROTOTYPE

Water-cooling and other technical improvements introduced the DT125LC for 1982, following in the tracks of the YZ models (above).

The RD125LC copied the style of the larger twins in a light, agile package.

The RD80MX kept the road format in an economy form with wire wheels and air-cooling.

Beluga extended the scooter range with a 79cc two-stroke engine and automatic transmission.

A YZ250 with water-cooled engine as for 1987, the change from air being made five years earlier.

The XJ900 in its original 1983 form with troublesome fairing, which was altered for the next year.

XVZ12TD

A massive tourer, the XVZ12TD Venture had a V-4 engine and was very well-equipped.

For riders preferring the two-stroke engine there was the RD500LC which was powered by a V-4 engine along the lines of the successful factory racer. The frame, suspension, fairing and finish all added to the race-replica style and the performance was exceptional.

Off-road, the big single was stretched out to 595cc to create the XT600 which continued with the two carburettors. A second version of the model was the XT600Z Ténéré which was a replica of the works Paris-Dakar machines so was fitted with a much larger petrol tank. The enduro range added the IT200 model to the others.

The RSX100 commuter two-stroke for 1983, which continued its traditional role.

A shaft drive scooterette, the T80 Town Mate, which had an overhead-camshaft engine (below).

XJ600

The XJ600 took over the middleweight role shared by two other models and came with fairing and belly pan.

Largest of the slim, four-cylinder range was the FJ1100, complete with fairing.

The RD500LC took the lines of the factory racer with a V-4 two-stroke engine.

RD500LC

For off-road use, the big single was stretched to the XT600 while retaining its features (below).

XT600

XT600Z TÉNÉRÉ

The Ténéré XT600Z copied the works models and came with a much larger fuel tank (above).

IT200

Enduro models such as this IT200 were based on the YZ range with lights and silencer added.

FIVE VALVES AND V-MAX 1985-1986

Yamaha engine technology took a step forward for 1985, with the introduction of an engine with five valves for each cylinder: three inlet valves and two exhaust valves. Additionally, the cylinders were inclined at a 45-degree angle and were fed their mixture by downdraught carburettors. The model was the FZ750 and it had an in-line, four-cylinder engine with twin camshafts and water-cooling.

The new engine concept moved the weight forward and down, and was matched by a new frame which kept the whole package slim, light and agile. The remainder of the machine added to its abilities and the firm had a new and successful trend.

For pure acceleration, riders in the United States were offered the V-Max. This took the engine from the Venture, uprated it, and fitted it in a much lighter machine, styled for impact. On the drag strips it was fast, but on the street the custom style made high speed hard work.

First of the new generation of sports Yamaha models was the FZ750 which introduced the inclined engine with five valves per cylinder.

The monster V-Max offered the massive V-4 engine, not too much weight, and tremendous style and performance.

A further variation in the four-stroke, trail-model theme was the XT350, which kept the lines and technology (above).

SRX600

Similar in concept to the SR500, the SRX600 of 1986 used the trail-model engine in a road chassis.

Far away, in Japan, the FZ theme progressed to the FZR400 to meet the demands for race replicas in the very popular 400cc class. In Europe, the XJ900 had a capacity increase, the Venture became a listed model and the off-road range was supplemented by the XT350 which had a twin-cam, four-valve engine and styling to match its larger brothers. At the bottom end of the scale came the MS50, an off-road moped which had a two-stroke engine, two-speed automatic transmission, and shaft drive. In addition to this, there was a 125cc version of the Beluga scooter to supplement the smaller edition.

A new style appeared for 1986 as the SRX600 which was based on the XT600 engine in a road format to hark back to the days of the single. The specification was modern, however, and the performance good. Additionally, for the custom rider there was the XV1000 Virago which replaced the TR1 and performed much better, while the FJ1200 took over from the 1100. A 50cc Town Mate joined the 80cc version while the enduro range was extended to include several models with a single-cylinder, four-stroke engine, these being listed as the TT225, TT250, TT350 and TT600.

The big V-twin custom model became the XV1000 Virago in 1986, stretching to this XV1100 two years later.

From 1986, the FJ1200 continued the lines of the smaller four that preceded it.

TT225

An enduro range powered by a four-stroke single joined the IT models and the smallest was this TT225.

TT350/250

For the mid-range there were TT250 and TT350 models; this was the smaller model.

TT600

Largest of the TT series was this 600, which followed the lines of the XT machines.

GENESIS AND DELTABOX 1987-1992

More super-sports models joined the Yamaha range for 1987, the most important of which was the FZR1000. This also took the 'Genesis' name which had been used, up to then, by the works YZF750 endurance racer, and which continued the concept of the well-inclined engine with five valves per cylinder, as used by the FZ750. The new model continued this theme using an aluminium frame, which was based on that of the endurance racer and the grand prix 500. This new frame had the top beams splayed round the cylinder head, was fitted with rising-rate rear suspension and massive front forks and took the name of 'Deltabox'.

The new frame type was also used by the TZR250, a new two-stroke twin based on the racing TZ250, which was a replacement for the smaller ageing Elsie. The engine retained many of the features from the racing unit, with minor amendments for road use, but the result was a natural for production racing, just as the RD series had been.

The FZR1000 introduced the Genesis series using the inclined, five-valve engine in a new frame.

Yamaha called their new aluminium frame Deltabox and based it on that used for racing.

New for 1987 in the Deltabox frame was the TZR250, continuing the line of two-stroke twins.

Custom cruising using the latest five-valve engine was the style of the FZX750.

For sports use, the FZ600 took the XJ600 engine but hid it under a fairing.

The firm took their new engine concept into the custom-cruiser world with the FZX750. This machine combined the inclined engine with some of the line of the Virago and V-Max. The FZ600 was another new sports model which came with a full fairing, but underneath this was the old XJ600 engine.

Early in the year the bottom end of the range saw the reappearance of the FS1 moped, still much as when it had first been the teenager's favourite, and the TZR125 which had a Deltabox frame in steel but painted as aluminium, a high-tech engine, and all the race style of the larger twin. For youngsters there were the PW50 and PW80 mini-bikes, built in motocross style using two-stroke engines. The smaller had automatic transmission, the larger three speeds, an automatic clutch and monoshock rear suspension.

A new custom V-twin appeared for 1988, the XV535. This model was built with an air-cooled, overhead-camshaft engine, shaft drive, and had the style and fittings expected of the type. For the trail came the TDR250 which was unusual in fitting the high-performance TZR250 twin two-stroke engine in an off-road chassis with the exhausts running high on each side. The DT125R took over from the earlier model with a much-revised engine based on the TZR125 in a new frame. For city use there was the CG50 Jog scooter, a compact model designed for easy operation and minimal maintenance.

Back from the past came the FS1, much as before with four speeds and drum brakes.

Styled for the young with a Deltabox frame, the TZR125 was also offered with a fairing.

Starting young could be by courtesy of a PW50 if your parents had a big garden.

Juniors could move on to the PW80 and a field in which to test their skill (below).

Harking back to the past, Yamaha introduced a retro model for its home market in Japan, the SR400. This used a single-cylinder, overhead-camshaft engine in a style reminiscent of the old British single. It proved to be a success.

The Genesis concept continued with two more models for 1989, one the FZR600 and the other the FZR750R, also listed as the OW01. Both of these were intended for racing but the first had to manage with a 16-valve engine which went into a Deltabox frame while the fixtures, fittings and finish were all as for the type. The OW01 was available with an optional parts kit for even higher track performance and was to continue to push the Yamaha to the front of the very competitive race class.

There were two other new models that year, one of these being the XTZ750 Super Ténéré which took the inclined engine, five-valve concept into the off-road area. The engine was a twin, with internal balancer shafts, and retained the water-cooling and downdraught carburettors. The frame was in steel, but used the Deltabox rear fork, while the fittings included a 26-litre petrol tank. The second new model was the XV1100 custom V-twin stretched out from the earlier Virago.

True custom low-rider style of the United States gave the XV535 its lines.

The unusual two-stroke twin trail model TDR250 harked back to the early Ascot and DS street scramblers.

Another step along the two-stroke trail line was this 1988 DT125R using the latest technology (below).

DT125R

BL2 (Black)

The CY50 Jog-In scooter was for city and suburban easy riding (above).

FZR600

The middleweight Genesis model was this FZR600 with Deltabox frame and fairing, but with only 16 valves for its 4 cylinders.

Built for racing, the FZR750R was also listed as the OW01 and had a specification which won races.

OW-01 FZR750R

The XTZ750 Super Ténéré used an inclined, five-valve, twin-cylinder engine to take the trail model to new levels (below).

Yet another scooter was added for 1990 as the CW50 B-Whizz, much on the lines of the Jog but with fatter tyres. The next year brought the FZR400RRSP, which was a further member of the Genesis family. First seen on the Japanese domestic market, this model had already won the Supersport 400 TT, fitted a 16-valve engine in a Deltabox frame and was in short supply in Europe with only an allocation of 100 for Britain.

New for 1991 were the XTZ660 Ténéré, which took over from the 600, and the TDM850 which, it was claimed, created a 'New Sports' category of machine. It continued the lines set by the XTZ750 in using the inclined, 10-valve, twin-cylinder engine, but in a Deltabox frame and equipped for road use. It was aimed at the rider who enjoyed cruising and corners, but had to cope with city traffic, so did not need either a race replica or a trail bike.

Yet another facet of Yamaha transport was the off-road quad, this example from 1995 (above).

DYGM1 (Deep Yellowish Green Metallic)

Fat tyres for the CW50 BW's scooter, later known as the B-Whizz.

FZR400RR SP

Another model built for racing, the FZR400RRSP had the inclined engine, Deltabox frame, but only four valves per cylinder (above).

The trail single grew some more for 1991 to become the XTZ660 Ténéré with a five-valve, single-cylinder engine.

Yamaha claimed that this TDM850 created a New Sports category with the ten-valve, twin-cylinder engine in a road chassis (above).

popularity has just kept on growing.

And over the years our engineers have made a series of detailed improvements that make the Yamaha FJ1200 one of the most reliable and refined sports tourers you'll ever ride.

Designed to effortlessly cover long distances at high speeds, the latest FJ offers unrivalled levels of rider and passenger comfort.

Yamaha FJ1200. Still running smooth and strong.

The FJ1200A model joined the stock one in 1991 and was fitted with ABS as standard.

WR250

The enduro model WR250 could be fitted with lights but continued to be based on the YZ range (above).

Smallest of the motocross models was this YZ80, seen here in its 1995 form.

The FJ1200A joined the stock sports tourer and – as a first for a Japanese production motorcycle – was fitted with ABS as standard. With electronic controls, it aided safety, while the standard version remained available. For enduro riders there was the WR250 which took over the job once done by the IT series. It kept the YZ motocross technology along with the necessary changes for its class of competition.

When the 1992 range appeared it was missing one very long-serving model, the YB100, which had been in production for close-on two decades. However, there was a good line of new models which would run along with the many that continued. These included the motocross range in YZ80, YZ125 and YZ250 forms, the road racing TZ125 and TZ250, the trials TY250 and the enduro WR250 which was joined by the WR200 and WR500. For the junior rider there came the RT100 trail model as a step up from a PW80.

The FZR400RR joined the super-sports range, its 16-valve engine in the Deltabox frame, but intended for road use while the SP version remained for competition. The XJ600 was replaced by the XJ600S Diversion which kept the existing air-cooled engine but inclined it forward some 35 degrees and installed it in a new chassis with a half fairing. The custom range saw the return of the XV750 in the style of the other V-twin models, and the scooter range added the XC125 which had a single-cylinder, overhead-camshaft engine and automatic transmission.

Next motocross model was the YZ125, ever improved in engine and chassis.

Road racing TZ models in 125 and 250cc sizes continued for many years. This one is from 1985 and minus the fairing.

RT100

The RT100 was introduced for the younger rider seeking to move on from a PW80.

FZR400RR

Very similar to its racing companion, the FZR400RR was intended for road use as a super-sports model.

XJ600

Sport and touring was the province of the XJ600S Diversion model, introduced for 1992 using old and new concepts.

In 1992 the XV750 returned to the range, much as before with its custom style (above).

XC125

The XC125 was a scooter with a four-stroke engine and a neat style.

OMEGA AND RETRO 1993-1996

T here were several important new models for 1993 and the most radical of these was the GTS1000, for this machine had a new front suspension system. This carried the wheel at the front of a single swinging arm with this linked to a pillar able to slide and turn within the headstock. The shape of the chassis gave rise to its name, Omega, and it carried the Genesis engine from the FZR1000. A full fairing was fitted and ABS was standard.

In the 125cc class there were two new models, one of them being the TZR125R which was based on the existing machine but had its frame inspired by the TZ250, better forks, bigger brakes and a full fairing in racing style. The second was the TDR125 which copied the 'New Sports' style of the TDM850, but with a two-stroke engine in a Deltabox frame.

New super-sports 750s replaced the FZ series with the YZF750R for the road and the YZF750SP for racing, for which a further tuning kit was available. Both continued the Genesis concept with an inclined 20-valve engine hung in a Deltabox frame. All areas were improved to keep them in competition in their class, which was hotly contested both on the track and in the showroom.

The GTS1000 introduced Yamaha's Omega chassis concept with a new suspension system and ABS as standard.

DRC2(Deep Red Cocktail 2)

Totally divorced from the track was the SR250 – much as the SR125, with a single-cylinder, overhead-camshaft engine and basic specification. The scooter range added the Zest, which was designed and built in Europe for the home market, and had a new chassis fitted with telescopic front forks.

Yamaha reacted to the fast-increasing retro market late in 1993 with the XJR400, only sold in Japan, and the huge XJR1200. This recalled the XS1100, having a 1188cc, four-cylinder, air-cooled, 16-valve, twin-cam engine inclined forward in a traditional style of frame with twin rear suspension units.

The XV535S joined the custom range for 1994, having extra chrome-plating and two-tone paint work to make it more striking than the stock model. The TT250R Rally Raid Special, based on the XT250, was offered for desert racing so had auxiliary petrol tanks, a water tank and other fittings to suit.

Close up of the new front suspension arm of the GTS1000.

TZR125R

The TZR125R used racing style and technology in a super-sports format which included the fairing.

VRC1 (Vivid Red Cocktail 1)

Urban motorcycling in Yamaha's New Sports style was the province of the TDR125.

The YZF750R was the road-going replacement for the FZ super-sports 750cc class in 1993.

For competition, the YZF750SP was listed with a further tuning kit to augment its tremendous performance.

Basic, but with a touch of custom style, the SR250 returned to drum brakes but kept the electric starting.

More models were added for 1995, continuing established themes. Thus, the XJ600N was the Diversion model less the fairing, while the new XJ900 Diversion was the old model plus a fairing. The XV250S took the custom style down to a smaller V-twin engine and the YZF600R followed the lines of the 750. The XT225 put a smaller model in the four-stroke trail range while the RT180 appeared as big brother to the RT100 and the TW200 was yet another four-stroke trail model, aimed more at the casual rider.

During 1995 the SZR660 brought in a new style by combining the trail-model engine, a little uprated, with the TZR250-type, Deltabox frame. Styled and developed in Italy, it offered good performance and excellent handling.

The Zest scooter was built in Europe for that market and styled to suit.

Tradition in the retro form brought the XJR1200 in 1993, recalling the XS1100 of the past.

The XV535S of 1994 continued the Virago line with extra chrome plating and a special paint job (above).

DCM 2 (Dark Cyan Metallic 2)

A larger Diversion, the XJ900S, appeared for 1995 to continue the theme and line.

RES (RED-E SPARKLE)

Smallest of the Virago series, the XV250S, was introduced for 1995 and retained the V-twin engine format.

The middleweight contender in Genesis form and Deltabox frame was this 1995 YZF600R (below).

YZF600R

The XT225 trail model was added to the four-stroke single range for 1995 (above).

A further step on from the PW80 and RT100 was this 1995 RT180.

TW200

The TW200 was another variant of the trail-model range with much fatter tyres (above).

Revised for 1996, the XC125TR Cygnus kept its four-stroke engine but gained telescopic front forks amongst its changes.

THE SZR660 was designed in Italy, first seen in 1995 and used the big trail-model engine.

There was a new style and much-revised engine for the 1996 version of the TDM850.

Late in the year the 1996 range was unveiled at the Paris show to introduce a good number of new and revised models. Largest was the XVZ1300A Royal Star, built in the custom mould, powered by a 1294cc water-cooled, V-four engine, but styled with cooling fins, which went into a chassis that reflected the early-postwar style while keeping a modern suspension system. Speedometer and clock were mounted in the tank top, the wheelbase was long and a massive range of accessories was listed.

Fastest of the 1996 range was the YZF1000R Thunder Ace which was all new, but followed existing Yamaha practice with an inclined, five-valve engine and Deltabox frame in a compact package. Similar, but smaller, was the YZF600R Thunder Cat seen in the 1995 United States' line, but without the name, and further developed.

The TDM850 engine was to a new design for 1996, while keeping to its ten-valve, twin cylinder format, for it had a 270-degree crankshaft and this resulted in an uneven power pulse and more torque. The chassis was revised to reduce the wheelbase and the bodywork restyled, the fairing carrying twin headlamps. The same engine was used for the TRX850, hanging it from a trellis frame which had a suspension system tailored to suit European riders and conditions. The result was quick and agile.

Scooter riders were not forgotten for 1996 with the advent of the YP250 Majesty, which was powered by a 249cc, four-stroke single driving a fully automatic V-belt transmission. Its chassis was advanced with telescopic front forks, adjustable rear suspension, disc front brake and drum rear, while the bodywork offered both comfort and three separate storage spaces.

Smaller was the XC125TR Cygnus, which offered revised bodywork styling, telescopic front forks and a front disc brake among its modifications. The smallest of the scooters was the BW's 50 B-Wizz. Along with several other changes, this machine was restyled in a radical manner which resulted in a new, fashionable line.

Top of the 1996 range was the XVZ1300A Royal Star with its older style, modern build and range of accessories.

Off-road, the Rally Raid was brought in as an enduro model, which was still listed as the TT250R, and the ranges of child's, trials and motocross models ran on as ever.

Thus, the extensive Yamaha model list grew, covering just about every aspect of motorcycling, whether for sport, touring or commuting. In addition, the firm has built many other forms of transport, for use on land or water, and also other products, all using engines in some way.

Meanwhile, music still continues to be played on high-quality Yamaha instruments, a constant reminder of the three tuning forks and the excellence that they represent.

New radical styling came to the BW's50 Bi-Wizz scooter for 1996, in order to change its image.

Top performer for 1996 was the YZF1000R Thunder Ace, which set new standards for its power, low weight, low drag and its compact dimensions.

Listed as an enduro model, rather than a desert racer, the TT250R came to Europe for 1996 (above).

The TRX850 used the new TDM850 engine hung from a trellis frame to create a new sports model.

Motocross models continued to be listed in 80cc, 125cc and this YZ250 form, thus continuing the long run of this successful series.

A new, sophisticated scooter for 1996 was this YP250 Majesty model which offered comfort and ease of use.

For the mid-range super-sports class, Yamaha listed the YZF600R Thunder Cat for Europe in 1996.

YAMAHA MODELS

No attempt will be made to list the hundreds of models built by Yamaha since 1954. Below are the basic types, most of which were built for several years, often with suffix codes to indicate minor changes. This would enable dealers to distinguish models to the year, aided by their parts lists and code numbers. The codes used prior to around 1970 have been omitted for clarity.

The lists that follow are arranged by engine cycle type, number of cylinders and intended purpose.

Two-strokes

Singles

Road	BW50, CA50, CG50, CW50, FS1E, MS50, QT50, RD50, SA50, T50, V50, V75, CV80, LB2-80, RD80LC, RD80MX, T80, V80, V90, RS100, RXS100, YB100, BL125, RD125LC, RS125, TDR125, TZR125, TZR125R
Trail	DT50, PW50, DT80, PW80, AG100, DT100, RT100, DT125, DT125LC, DT125R, DT175, RT180, TW200, DT250, DT360, DT400
Motocross	YZ80, MX100, YZ100, MX125, YZ125, MX250, YZ250, MX360, YZ360, MX400, YZ400
Trial	TY50, TY80, TY175, TY250
Enduro	IT125, IT175, IT200, WR200, IT250, WR250, IT400, IT425, IT465, IT490, WR500
Racing	TZ125

Twins

Road	RD125, RD200, RS200, RD250, RD250LC, TZR250, RD350, RD350LC, RD400
Trail	TDR250
Racing	TD2, TR2, TZ250, TZ350
Road Fours	RD500LC

Four Strokes

Singles

Road	XC125, XC125TR, SR250, YP250, SR400, XJR400, SR500, SRX600, SZR660
Custom	SR125SE, SR250SE
Trail	XT125, XT200, XT225, XT250, XT350, HL500, TT500, XT500, XT550, XT600, XT600Z, XTZ660
Enduro	TT225, TT250, TT250R, TT350, TT600

Twins

Road	XS250, XS250C, XS360, XS400, TX500, XS500, XZ550, XS1, XS2, XS650, TX750, TDM850, TRX850
Custom	XS250SE, XV250S, XS400SE, XV535, XV535S, XS650SE, XV750, XV750SE, TR1, XV1000, XV1100
Trail	XTZ750

Triples

Road	XS750, XS850
Custom	XS750SE

Fours

Road	FZR400, FZR400RR, FZR400RRSP, XJ550, FZ600, FZR600, XJ600, XJ600N, XJ600S, YZF600R, XJ650, XJ650 turbo, FZ750, FZR750R, XJ750, YZF750R, YZF750SP, XJ900, XJ900S, FZR1000, GTS1000, YZF1000R, FJ1100, XS1100, XS1100S, FJ1200, XJR1200, XVZ12TD
Custom	FZX750, V-Max, XVZ1300A